Thank you for choosing this book,

Mihaela Dodan

Dedication:
With love, to Lyra Arabella
and all the children who say

I'll do it myself!

ISBN-13: 978-0-9983518-0-3
ISBN-10: 0-9983518-0-3
Library of Congress Control Number: 2016918549

www.mihaeladodan.com
www.magicmindcollection.com

Magic Luggage

The Gift of Knowledge and Skills

Mommy, can you show me how to
draw a butterfly? Asked Lyra
Of course, said mommy.
Oh that's so cute, said Lyra.
Mommy, how can I draw a butterfly?
Asked Lyra.

This question will take you in a magic luggage adventure.

Are you ready for it? Asked mommy.
Yesss, said Lyra excitedly.

Do you remember when I showed you
on the map, the country
where I was born?
Yes, Romania, and when you grew up
you moved to America, said Lyra.

ROMANIA,
EUROPA

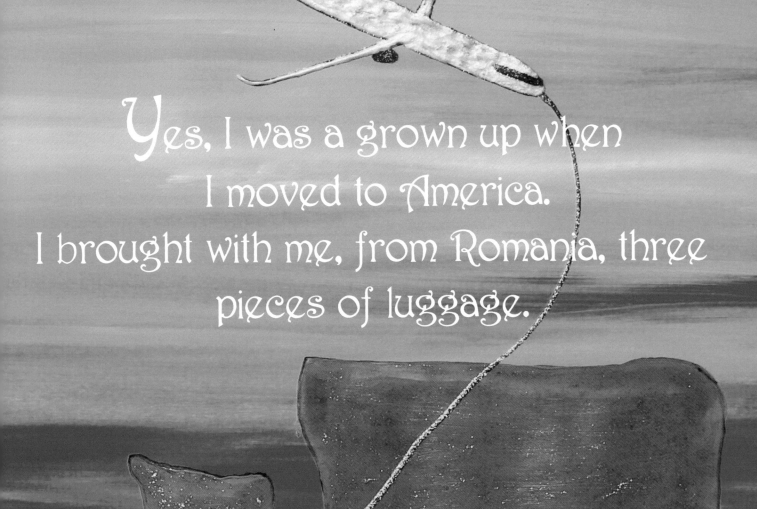

Yes, I was a grown up when
I moved to America.
I brought with me, from Romania, three
pieces of luggage.

WASHINGTON,
USA

The first luggage was big and overweight. It was full of things (clothes, shoes, books and some cosmetics).
I don't have anything left from that luggage.
Material things come and go.

The second luggage was small.
It had my travel documents and my
diplomas, snacks for the trip, a book
and a lipstick.

I read the book, I ate my food
and I used the lipstick.
I still have my documents and diplomas.

The third luggage was magic, sparkly and invisible. It's the most important luggage I brought with me. It's lighter than a feather and it follows me everywhere I go. I still have everything I had in that luggage and it keeps growing all the time.

What do you mean by magic luggage?
I want to have one too!
Said Lyra.

All the people have one and you already started to grow yours.
It's filled with all the skills you learn and it keeps growing because you keep learning every day.

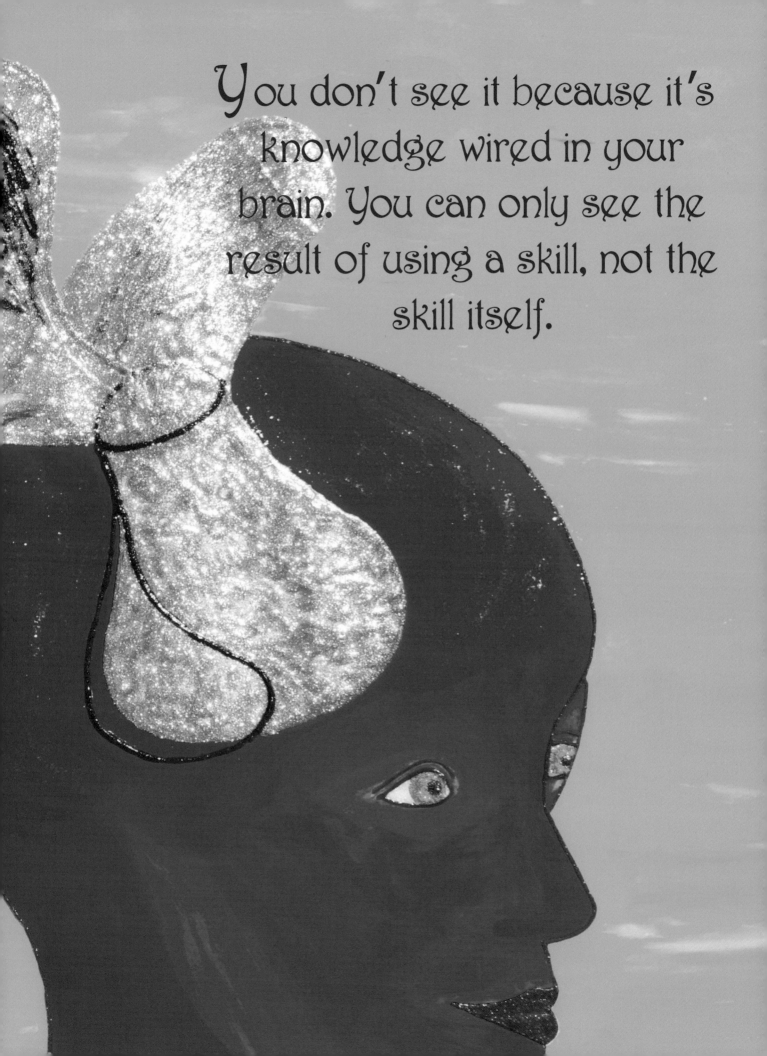

You don't see it because it's knowledge wired in your brain. You can only see the result of using a skill, not the skill itself.

Ski... what? What? asked Lyra
Skills, said mommy.
A skill is the ability to do something.
Ablitily... what? asked Lyra again.
A-bil-i-ty, said mommy slowly.
Ability means that you are able to do
something.

You know that babies don't walk
and as they grow, they learn
how to walk.
They start to roll over, then sit up and
crawl and so on until they walk.
Walking is a skill most people learn and
it's invisibly wired in the brain.

Writing is also a skill that almost anyone can acquire trough learning and practicing. Drawing a butterfly is very similar to writing "butterfly".

People who can draw learned to do it step by step and now you're learning too. Before you know it, your butterflies will be ready to fly off of the page, said mommy.

Some of the skills a person can learn are: Cooking, Cleaning, Gardening, Reading, Writing, Drawing, Painting,

Playing the piano, Driving, Tailoring, Sculpting, Ceramics, Jeweler, Inventing, Singing, Communications and more.

The more skills you learn,
the more independent you become.
A beautiful side of it is that no one can
take away from you this magic luggage.

It comes with you wherever you go
and whatever happens.
You use it, when you need it.

I want the astronaut skill, said Lyra.
Astronaut is a profession and it requires
many skills, said mommy smiling.
And I want the skill of cooking so that
I can make chocolate, said Lyra.
Every day chocolate!
By the time you will learn how to cook,
I'll teach you about Magic Nutrients that
your body needs to grow
strong and healthy, said mommy.

What skills would you like to learn?

What would you like to add to your magic luggage?

About Mihaela

I was born and raised in Romania with my four brothers during a very dark Communist era. I learned (often by the light of a candle) from cooking, cleaning, knitting, babysitting, how to open a can with a knife before I was seven to all the disciplines children learn in school.

At 22, after graduating college, I left Romania to work on cruise ships. That was an intense training on how to communicate with passengers; take care of their luggage and quarters; deal with paperwork and safety in a floating city; and manage countless other duties.

After five years of work aboard ships, I built a farm in Romania, I participated in building a meat-processing factory, and I started a publishing company.

Despite all this experience, I found myself not understanding the purpose of life. Wondering about it all, I set myself on a whole new course of learning, unlearning, and self-revealing.

In 2006, while still in Europe, I began to learn and practice energy healing techniques, Hypnosis, Neuro-Linguistic Programming (NLP), Mind Control, Life and Business Coaching, Health Coaching, and more. In 2010 I moved to the United States to study at RSE, in Yelm, WA. I have become even more passionate to know about the power of mind over matter.

In 2014 I graduated from the Institute of Integrative Nutrition, NY, as a Health Coach.

Somewhere in between I discovered my passion for writing and painting.

Lyra Arabella is a fairly new citizen of Planet Earth. Like all citizens on this planet, she will be taught how to navigate and live her life. I, her mommy, decided to create a series of short and simple books to pass on to Lyra, and those who find it useful, what I have learned so far.

Acknowledgements:
I am deeply grateful to
all of my teachers!

Other Magic Books in this collection:

Magic Choices

To be published:

Magic Chocolate

Magic Thoughts

Magic Words

Magic Nutrients

Magic Questions

Magic Invisibility

Magic Resources

And More

CPSIA information can be obtained at www.ICGtesting.com
Printed in the USA
BVIW12n0935281216
472005BV00002B/11